Summary
of

Make Your Bed: Little Things That Can Change Your Life...And Maybe the World
William H. McRaven

Conversation Starters

By BookHabits

Tips for Using BookHabits Conversation Starters:

EVERY GOOD BOOK CONTAINS A WORLD FAR DEEPER THAN the surface of its pages. The characters and their world come alive through the words on the pages, yet the characters and its world still live on. Questions herein are designed to bring us beneath the surface of the page and invite us into the world that lives on. These questions can be used to:

- Foster a deeper understanding of the book
- Promote an atmosphere of discussion for groups
- Assist in the study of the book, either individually or corporately
- Explore unseen realms of the book as never seen before

About Us:

THROUGH YEARS OF EXPERIENCE AND FIELD EXPERTISE, from newspaper featured book clubs to local library chapters, *BookHabits* can bring your book discussion to life. Host your book party as we discuss some of today's most widely read books.

Table of Contents

Introducing *Make Your Bed: Little Things That Can Change Your Life...And Maybe the World*

WILLIAM H. MCRAVEN IS A RETIRED UNITED STATES NAVY admiral whose last dates of service were August 2011 to August 2014. He has served as a chancellor of the University of Texas System since January 2015. McRaven's 2014 commencement speech went viral on YouTube, adding to his list of accomplishments a uniqueness that was followed by his novelization of the values he spoke about. McRaven's work, influenced by his time in the U.S. Navy, appeals to many for its military values and references to making hard decisions. His specific style of weaving anecdotes with encouragement and practicality offers a fresh perspective that made his speech incredibly popular. "Make Your Bed: Little Things That Can Change Your Life...And Maybe the World" presents readers with a series of stories that are both McRaven's and those of people he encountered during his service. It combines a reflective quality with support to share the author's desire for readers to achieve success.

McRaven's novel begins with a preface that is humble and motivational in nature. As the author explains, he was pleasantly shocked by the reception of his 2014 commencement speech. He believed his experience as a military officer might not translate well to a group of college graduates; however, he was proved wrong when the speech quickly became a hit. In the preface, the author details the universality of his experiences and how ten lessons have helped shape his life. He expands on the speech given at UT Austin, describing specific encounters with strangers and friends and how they helped prove the impact of each lesson. A chapter is dedicated to each lesson, from "Start Your Day with a Task Completed" to "Rise to the Occasion" and "Give People Hope". The very first lesson, "Start Your Day with a Task Completed", holds the argument for making one's bed every day. The author explains in vivid detail his service aboard the USS *Grayback* and how he made his bed each morning- a task that was not praised but expected. His striking tale of life in the Navy and his struggle with being unable to help during the attacks on 9/11 support his assertion that a simple task such as making one's bed can come to mean much more in life. McRaven's simple explanations and supportive tone characterize much of the book, proving his voice as one of reason and encouragement. As readers are faced with harrowing tales and heartfelt retellings of some of the author's most difficult challenges in life, they are also given the hope and push needed to expect more from themselves in life. The book certainly does its job as a motivational, self-help novel, using a comfortable and casual voice to discuss hard lessons that are sometimes very serious and impactful.

A second-time author and first-time casual novelist, McRaven's "Make Your Bed" is almost entirely a departure from most of the work in his life. His use of personal experience to promote a better lifestyle and success are, however, informed in great part by his military career. The author's novel thus relies on morals and ideals that might be unfamiliar to the audience yet are still universal enough to provide a clear image of the author's intent. "Make Your Bed" is an inspirational read, fulfilling the purpose of a step-by-step guide that encourages reflection and change. Readers of all ages and demographic have enjoyed the novel, reviewing and praising it as a moving narrative with implementable steps and clear benefits.

Discussion Questions

"Get Ready to Enter a New World"

Tip: Begin with questions dealing with broader issues to ensure ample time for quality discussions. Read through all discussion questions before engaging.

~~~

question 1

The author uses specific experiences within the U.S. Navy. Do you think these are successfully touching? Why or why not? Do they work as examples?

~~~

~~~

question 2

As McRaven explains, making one's bed can sometimes be more significant than completing a simple act. Do you agree with this characterization? Why or why not?

~~~

~~~

question 3

McRaven mentions in the prologue and novel that he has experience with others telling him about their decisions in life to face challenges. Do you think the experiences of others are added well in the narrative? Do they flow with the rest of the story? Why or why not?

~~~

~~~

question 4

The author mentions some very significant military operations throughout the book, one of which is Saddam Hussein's detainment by U.S. forces. Do you find these allusions jarring or off-putting? Why or why not? Do they somehow give the author credibility?

~~~

~~~

question 5

The ninth chapter in the novel is titled "Give People Hope". What do you think of McRaven's approach to doing this? Is it practical? Why or why not? Would you follow his outline?

~~~

~~~

question 6

The author speaks heavily about relying on the support of others. "You Can't Go It Alone" emphasizes this point. What is your opinion of the author's characterization of asking for or expecting support? Is it realistic? Why or why not?

~~~

~~~

question 7

As you read each of McRaven's anecdotes, are you able to relate to them? Why or why not?

~~~

~~~

question 8

One of the chapters in the book discusses how to learn and grow from failures. Do you agree with McRaven's characterization of failure? Why or why not? Is his approach to learning from mistakes common, or new? Does it work?

~~~

~~~

question 9

The author includes his commencement speech, which is a large part of his motivation for writing the novel. What is your opinion of the speech? Does it align well with the book?

~~~

~~~

question 10

Many of the stories in the book are anecdotes from either McRaven's experience or the experience of those he is familiar with. Do you think they make the author's argument stronger? Why or why not?

~~~

~~~

question 11

The author expresses surprise at the positive reception he received for his commencement speech. Do you agree? What qualities, in your opinion, made the speech and resulting novel so popular?

~~~

~~~

question 12

Some might argue that specific 'lessons' such as "Life's Not Fair" and "Stand Up to Bullies" are common assertions. Do you think the author does anything to make them his own? How? Is McRaven successful in creating an original narrative, or does it feel rehashed and familiar?

~~~

~~~

question 13

There is no clear, specific market audience for this novel. Do you think this hurts or helps the book? Why? Once you begin to read, do you think there is an audience that would enjoy it more? Why?

~~~

~~~

question 14

Do you agree with the author's assertion that starting your day with a success, no matter how small, can motivate one to do more? Why or why not? Is it in any way idealistic? Would you implement his suggestion?

~~~

~~~

question 15

The stories in the novel take place during different times in the author's life. Do you think the novel flows well despite this? Why or why not? Does it feel natural or do the shifts break your concentration and immersion in the novel?

~~~

~~~

question 16

"Make Your Bed" was written after the author's viral speech at UT Austin.
Do you think it was a good idea to novelize the lessons McRaven spoke
about? Why or why not?

~~~

~~~

question 17

The novel is praised and recommended by some for "every leader in America". Do you agree with this proposed target audience? Why or why not? Give specific chapter examples from the book.

~~~

~~~

question 18

McRaven was involved in Operation Neptune Spear, which was a raid that led to the death of Osama bin Laden. His presence in the U.S. military is enormous. Do you think this comes through in the book? How so? Does it help or hurt the narrative?

~~~

~~~

question 19

Each chapter of the book includes anecdotes to supplement the lessons being described. Aside from stories, what do you think could have made McRaven's argument stronger? Would it be necessary to include other examples, or does the book succeed as it is?

~~~

~~~

question 20

The book is divided into sections by lessons. Do you feel each of them are well-organized? Would you be able or willing to follow them? Do you think that is the author's intent?

~~~

Introducing the Author

WILLIAM HARRY MCRAVEN IS A 1977 GRADUATE OF THE University of Texas at Austin. He graduated with a bachelor's degree in journalism and obtained a master's degree from the Naval Postgraduate School. McRaven's periods of duty include June 2006 to March 2008, June 2008 to August 2011, and August 2011 to August 2014. His military career has been marked by service in Joint Special Operations Command, Special Operations Command Europe, and United States Special Operations Command. McRaven retired in August of 2014 after over 37 years of service. Much of his life and career has been marked by a dedication to achievement and a recognition of the necessity to do more in difficult situations. As a speaker and author, McRaven often calls on his military experience for examples of how living life to achieve more has benefitted both himself and others. The author's openness and direct recounting of harrowing events has characterized him in the public sphere as a straightforward and motivational individual.

Outside of his military career, McRaven is a dedicated father of three children. He has described his dedication to helping others through his experiences and how "Make Your Bed: Little Things That Can Change Your Life...and Maybe the World" is meant to describe how "ten lessons shaped [his] life". As a writer, McRaven is humble and highly descriptive, captivating readers with vivid retellings of life lessons he has experienced. The author is influenced by his children and his wife, Georgeann, whom he asserts have made his life better. As a first-time author of a commercial novel, McRaven has enjoyed positive reviews and praise for his unique voice and dedication to helping others through his experiences.

McRaven published his novel "Make Your Bed" in April 2017. His continued involvement in the public sphere has made him a prominent figure in American society. The use of anecdotes and significant military experiences in his novel has forged a connection between the author and readers of both military and non-military backgrounds. Many lovers of motivational and self-help writing have eagerly awaited the novel, citing the author's commencement speech as proof of his capability to capture audience attention. McRaven is a prolific and prominent member of the military community, making him a vital voice and interesting narrator of motivational nonfiction.

Fireside Questions

"What would you do?"

Tip: These questions can be a fun exercise as it spurs creativity among the readers by allowing alternate scene endings and "if this was you" questions.

~~~

question 21

McRaven has spent most of his life in military positions. Do you think this affects his writing voice? In what way?

~~~

~~~

question 22

The author's first degree was in journalism. Is this apparent in the book? How so? Do you think it gives him an advantage in writing? Why?

~~~

~~~

question 23

McRaven has never written a novel for the public in this vein before. Do you think this is apparent? Why? Do you think he could write another book that would be well-received?

~~~

~~~

question 24

While the author was involved in high-profile military operations, the details are not entirely released to the public. Do you feel that the author's voice makes up for some vague points in his narrative? In what way?

~~~

~~~

question 25

The novel focuses on helping the reader better themselves using examples from personal experiences. Is it successful in the use of these anecdotes? How?

~~~

~~~

question 26

In the beginning of the novel, the author describes how others questioned him about his experience and growth using ten lessons. Do you believe his motivation to write the novel as an answer to these questions? Why or why not? Is it successful in answering the questions?

~~~

~~~

question 27

J Some of McRaven's stories involve difficult decisions. Do you believe the author is trustworthy, based on the decisions? Why or why not? Would you have acted differently?

~~~

~~~

question 28

The author is very specific in his discussion about how completing a simple task- such as making one's bed- can become groundwork for success. Would you have used this example? Why or why not? What is another way you may have explained the principle?

~~~

~~~

question 29

Many of the experiences in the book revolve around the author's military career. What would you have used for context if you wrote the book? Why? Would you change it at all?

~~~

~~~

question 30

At the beginning of the book, the author quickly sets a specific tone. What do you think it is? Would you have chosen a different tone? Why or why not?

~~~

Quiz Questions

"Ready to Announce the Winners?"

Tip: Create a leaderboard and track scores to see who gets the most correct answers. Winners required. Prizes optional.

~~~

quiz question 1

"Make Your Bed: Little Things That Can Change Your Life...And Maybe
the World" was written primarily to help people
_____ by using the author's experiences. It
speaks heavily about the importance of motivation.

~~~

~~~

quiz question 2

The novel focuses on using _____ as examples, which makes it relatable to many people. The stories are from the author's personal experiences.

~~~

~~~

quiz question 3

The author attempts to _____ the reader. This is apparent in many chapters; especially the one targeted towards learning from mistakes.

~~~

~~~

quiz question 4

True or False: The author's book is not entirely nonfiction, as it revolves around a character based on his experiences.

~~~

~~~

quiz question 5

True or False: McRaven has written novels before. This makes him more qualified to recount his experiences for the benefit of others.

~~~

quiz question 6

True or False: The novel is divided into chapters by lesson. This makes it easy to follow and implement in one's life.

~~~

~~~

quiz question 7

True or False: All of the stories in the novel are other people's experiences. As a journalist, McRaven exclusively interviewed others to create the narrative for the book.

~~~

~~~

quiz question 8

McRaven is a graduate of _____ ___, where he gave his famous commencement speech in 2014. He serves as a chancellor for the school.

~~~

~~~

quiz question 9

The author's service in _____ influenced a
great deal of his book. Many of his anecdotes relate to military life.

~~~

~~~

quiz question 10

F"Make Your Bed" was released in 2017, several years after _____ went viral. The author did not expect the positive response to his speech and decided to write the book to answer people's questions.

~~~

quiz question 11

True or False: McRaven is a professor at UT Austin, which is in part due to his speech. This book was written for his class.

~~~

quiz question 12

True or False: While McRaven has written a book about Special Operations before, this is his first commercial publication. It has already been received well.

~~~

Quiz Answers

1. change their lives
2. anecdotes
3. motivate
4. False
5. False
6. True
7. False
8. The University of Texas at Austin
9. the United States Navy
10. his 2014 commencement speech
11. False
12. True

Ways to Continue Your Reading

EVERY month, our team runs through a wide selection of books to pick the best titles for readers and reading groups, and promotes these titles to our thousands of readers – sometimes with free downloads, sale dates, and additional brochures.

Want to register yourself or a book group' It's free and takes 1-click.

Register here.

On the Next Page...

Please write us your reviews! Any length would be fine but we'd appreciate hearing you more! We'd be SO grateful.

Till next time,

BookHabits

"Loving Books is Actually a Habit"

Made in United States
Orlando, FL
29 September 2023

37424482R00035